NO ARCADIA

NO ARCADIA

D. Eric Parkison

JANE'S BOY PRESS

        Jane's Boy Press
        219 Arlington Street
        Watertown, NY 13601

        www.janesboypress.com

Typeset, internal & cover design by Kiel M. Gregory

Text set in Adobe Garamond Pro

Manufactured in the United States of America

First Edition
Jane's Boy Press, August 2020

ACKNOWLEDGMENTS

I would like to thank the following publications in which these poems originally appeared, some in slightly different form:

B O D Y
"Winter Cropland"

Columbia Review
"Asymptote"

Crab Creek Review
"Little Katabasis"

Low Valley Review
"Transmission"
"Wood Stove"

SpoKe 5
"Oh, Oh, Oh"
"Staying Over" appearing as "Equinox Sequence"
"Not Asleep, Not Awake"

Squaw Valley Review
"Pierce-Arrow Limousine"

The Tishman Review
"The Common"

Zyzzyva
"Perfect House"

CONTENTS

I

II

III

Then I walked on and crossed the bridge.

— Seamus Heaney, "An Advancement of Learning"

I

NOT ASLEEP, NOT AWAKE

In summer the one air conditioner
Is shared: you sleep on the floor
In the air-conditioned room. His silence.
His room. You wake because there's a presence
Before he starts. See the curtain, the pale
Moon. Again, his breathing. Each inhale,

Pulls deep, like collecting burrs drawing a bull-nose plane
Along fresh boards of white pine.
Like pulling off soft strips of birch bark.
When he begins again, you cinch your breath
To his. Sleep, his dominion. His country.
You, at the edge of a cool wood. Go in.

LITTLE KATABASIS

The harrow's rows of roller discs
Are tacky with a dark mortar:
Long grasses, clay, and black
Loam, dewfall-wetted. The tractor,
Off a quarter-hour, smells hot.

Deer eyes shine in this outer world.
Raccoons shuffle fatly,
Brown bats begin to tumble overhead.
To traipse this shorn landscape,
To watch, under a deflating sun,

Ashes scatter from bulldozed piles
Of brush, broken roots,
Pine boles ringed with broken branches,
Is to trespass.
Trespass, to watch smoke

Drift over the black pond.
Each wisp unravels, barrel-rolls
Into soft pills, then nothing. Swallowed
Water. The wood hisses, turning to embers
Under a grey crosshatch of contrails.

NATURAL LAWS

We cut the vine off at the ground
And said *this is liberation.*
Pushed off with the vine
Clutched in our hands.

Its dead fingers let go the branches
And we crash landed
On a wet bank thick with ferns.
This was our generation:

The failures from which we learned
Made it easy to stay down and cry.
Made it hard to stand.

ASYMPTOTE

Sometimes the hole's been dug before the birth.

What to do with the shirt.

Mothballs. Consignment. It covers. Things
Come before any of their names.

Sometimes a lease is backdated,
The house smolders,

Smoke slouches in the doorways.

Use a stool, step up
On the couch: out there, the silvered bark

Of the tree breaks
Above the shallow roots and curls up.

The tree climbing into its own branches

Is fluked with bark, is feathered.

At the nock-end
Of the arrow, the earth
Is the bowstring, stomped taut beneath the feet

Of its circling inhabitants, who one
After the other lighten the burden, leap away.

Loose arrow, knock a hole
In the belly-flesh of heaven: scatter

The ripe souls back into this mess.

How the crows manage on just their one word.

WOOD STOVE

Birds braid their nests into
Our old clay-lipped chimney.

There's a papery rustle in the flue
When they collapse into the heat,
The chirps of their last panic—

Withered feathers, skulls,
Remainders among the cinders,
Raked from the cleanout door.

No tacky gum of yolk and soot,
No soft-hued shells strewn like flakes of paint.

I work my finger into a clenched
Passerine claw,
Stroke, once, the tiny length of back,
Toss the gauzy bundle into the woods.

GARBAGE MAN

The knock of the woodpecker
Low on the trunk speeds up, quits; the muscles

Await its beginning again. Soon, the loose wire
Of a cicada bites the air between walnut trees

Which drop their green pods—one thump,
Two—arrhythmic plod of a Bacchus

Or satyr. Would his sweet tea turn wine,
Stiffer stuff: gin, evergreen distillate

To keep him here in his dream:
A life of discernment, sure-footedness,

Measured choices—to carry him away
From his violet-lidded fatigue,

His repetitions: the can is full, he lifts,
he tips, the can is empty, acrid urine,

Dry rain of spent litter. This morning,
The sunrise was like a cut plum

Behind one of the nice houses
—Soft firs lined their half circle of blacktop,

Their dog bounded up beside him—
And a college girl, in her jean shorts—

Walking, always, away. The fresh paint…
His cigarettes smell to him like bran flakes

When he opens them, it puffs out
On that heel-of-the-hand tap-*tap*,

And he sits in his chair,
The buzz of mosquitoes, his favorite cup—

Go Bills!—and he learns
To be pliant again, he ends at rest:

Is the earth empty? He feels it is,
He is lonely as God—he is all.

II

STAYING OVER

We played with the rotary dial on the pink phone,
Lifted the earpiece from its mount on the cupboard.
His mother turned on the tap, which choked
And sputtered, spitting bay water into the pan.

Then, he rolled an egg along the checkered
Tablecloth, delicate as a sphere of dried paint. *This*
He said, *is the one day of the year this*
Will work. At attention, broad shouldered,

The egg stood on tippy toes. Science or art,
For him it didn't matter.
Same difference. That night, top bunk, I had
      a dream

I wrenched out my teeth. I took my mouth apart,
Rolled from the mattress in terror,
Afraid I'd cracked my head along its fresh seam.

A PERMANENT GARMENT

The fork with the heavy wrist
Rests in the tack
Of a messy plate.
Tines toward three
If it were the face of a clock...

Endlessness has a slow way
Of happening. The routine
Failure of each hour. One day,
The next. Begun, breakfasted, done.

Salt-flecked potato bits
Take their time and rest
Among the limp red onions,
Harassment over. Little wonders.

The OJ seems sour,
The milk expired in accordance
With its purple date. The placemat.
A cubicle. A window:

All the power in being able
To be someone else. An enticement
Nice to envision. Impossible—
Like a permanent garment,
Or the best utensil, its perfect placement.

THE COMMON

The dignity of being consistent:
One goose, and then the others,
All hiss at us but eat the bread,

The black eyes blink in each black head.
Across the water, in the trees, the wind stirs.
I loved you after I didn't.

ALLIED TERRITORY

Wet clover and patches of grass would grow
To nag the driveway stones and call the bees
To interrupt our games of pig or horse.
They'd spread like stains each spring, go orange and white
With flowers, breaking what I thought was one
Idea into many disparate things:

A proof that what we planned would always fail.
The plain on which our first campaigns were launched—
With water guns or gasoline or sticks
We would begin our march against the nests.
The place where fathers came to pick us up
Against our wills each Friday afternoon.

The driveway to the farmhouse where we lived,
Near the north end of a road with two names,
Outside a town too small to make a noise
When Durkees closed, or Nixons' roof collapsed—
All those insurgencies of weeds and grass
Could stand for that as well: they shouldered up

Between the stones, occupied the edges
To prove our claims had been provisional.
A stubborn boy might pry out clumps of grass
By kicking at the dirt on autumn days
When darkness follows close the morning sun,
Or slam a basketball against one spot,

But come next spring the grass will grow again,
And the plow guy, who came all winter long,
A helpful neighbor from just down the street,
Will have pushed the bigger stones into the yard:
A further blurring of the boundary line,
The delaying action masking a retreat.

THRASH

Home from his last tour, the old man eyes me cautiously
From the table where he stays. He strikes if I come close.

     The state crews are out all night
          knocking down the toxic hogweed.

I pass through the screen door, walk into the orchard.
I start my truck out back of Spencers' barn.

     The road I pop up onto
          is dark and lined with hogweed.

Ropey sealant glistens, snaking in the headlights.
Furnace Road goes through the countryside.

     I take the truck along a field:
          it's turned, and edged with hogweed.

The soybean sprouts drink up the irrigation.
This love plus suffering is some new season.

     The brake lights light the billowed dust,
          red as blisters from the hogweed.

Deer plunge into the night, hop each ridge and furrow:
Their thrash is plain reaction: it's that or else the vultures eat.

     Big rocks in piles at each end of the field,
          dusted white as all the hogweed.

I want to be handsome, not to be a better man,
And there's no way to master such a broken thing.

     The stones that ping the oil pan
          spring off into the hogweed.

AUBADE

No big star, no burst of rays
Breaking from behind the hills.
They lope in silhouette still,
Move through mist into place.

Weird distance in the groves of black trees:
Short oaks armored in lichen:
The scalloped petals in constellations
Along the limbs. Not our property.

Last night, in with a crack of pistol-fire,
The moon shone, our bodies gleamed.
Others emerged from shadows
Shedding their clothes.

We followed flashlights
Over rows of young grapes—opaque bunches
Of frog-eggs, god-eggs, dewy, green—
We joined the carousal, watched

The ridged muscles of a pale leg
Disappear to the knee, receding
Into the audible murk of the pond.
You and I on shore with our whistles.

This morning, your breath burns away what's left
Of the dark. I crawl from our tent, penitent
in the purple quarter-light of not-yet dawn.
I am supposed to wake you and will not.

PERFECT HOUSE

I'm thinking about how I could keep the perfect house.

Now I can keep the perfect house.

I'm watching sunlight dapple things, boring things.
Now, the things are dappled by sunlight.

Carefully, one puts word and word down
      In procession: one insists

That the order of the words will lead you through them.
      I do not believe

That the procession of words will save us.
I'm looking at stacked books I've piled

On tables and shelves. Tables and shelves

In my house are static with books. I'm thinking about how
I could keep the perfect house. Wondering

What's all this being said, now? Now, I'm wondering what
I've said. Three journals made of cardstock. An anthology

Of poetry. A manila folder, coffee stain too suggestive
To happen, but there, and thinking *the folder*

With the stain is right: the stain mounded like
Recently tattooed skin, the edges scrunched and fraying.

I thought I'd come here for a reason.
There is no reason. I'm thinking what the reason could be.

I can't think of a reason.

I HAVE BEEN AT THIS CORNER

1

The blooded copper crowns of the pine stand
Waiver on the edge a farmer cut into the hillside
With a power shovel, a bucket, to set in two more rows
Of some fruit-bearing tree, and to the west

The watery orange disc sizzles in the clouds.
The dog is grimfaced on her leash, she pulls
After the trail of some carrion or trash.

A diaper, as it happens, taped down
Into a permanent summersault, tucking out of view
The greased slick of who knows whose kid.
Difficult, here, to make hope of scant things.

Across the vaster orchard of the down slope,
Two pole barns stand, awaiting the season's start.

Something old about them, out-buildings, inheritors
Of the temple shapes of Greece. Maybe Wordsworth

Would reprimand the local folks
For the angle and stagger: they offset
A sense of balance, staked and cabled
In among spear-shaft saplings.

I walk inattentive and dumb,
Not quite to the middle, yet, of the track
We have fallen into: practice repeated is ritual.

Earlier, the boy laughed, charged off
With a handsaw while the man snored
From the couch. It took all I had to keep up.

2

How often I've slowed
In passing this place to look over the slop

And unruly guts of that pasture, hungry
For its scent and the sound of wind in it,
Its life, its patience like that of the resigned man
Resting in sweatpants
While his vision goes, the horse doctor

Clipping at his toenails, now he can't bend.
The trailer at the hill's crest squats
Like a tentacled thing, paths of scrap and truck tires
Snaking from the cinderblock steps at the front door.

Fence posts of rot-softened hawthorn
Or twisted oak wood strung with one
Rusting wire looks like they scuttled the whole project
In a barrage of swampy springs:

That's what echoes the corner lot's verge
Here where two roads cross, in the shadow
Of a stunted hill. Dumb cows crop the herbs
That bristle out beneath gray stones like dirty hair

From beneath a ball cap.
I don't know what to say: if it's a farm
Or place or what, or where the people keep
The grain—the base of a block silo

Like my granddad helped put up around the county
Sustains a few feet of curved wall
That make the thing look like a seat or throne
For some messy cyclopean beast, the aluminum
Roof settled like a giant blossom beside it.

3

North from here, good bullhead fishing at dark,
South, the shuttered medical center
Where the children's records were destroyed, so much time
Passed between their shots
And when they needed to go—and besides,
No facilities for broken bones.

East, into Red Creek, named for
The tanner mill's spillage when
It was here a hundred years ago.

                      I've been at this corner
Many nights, many times, but how to say what's west?
The foundation of a house the first villager
Painted black to make it equal to his spirit,

The sunset, the man who sells potatoes
From the side door of his barn,
The scatter of satellite dishes, the orchard—

It seems that standing here everything is west.
And that this place, the mucky pond,
And the barefoot kid being chased
By his sister on the driveway,

That the mutt, and the potbellied father
Adjusting his hat at the mossy table,

Is just everything that's left.

III

ON VISITING WITH A HIGH SCHOOL
FRIEND

We walked the woods where we'd been young
To smell the spruce and autumn's chill,
And climbed the roots slung rung by rung
Across the trail up a steep hill,

Marveled at all that'd stayed the same
And walked back by the way we came,
Took off our boots and put on shoes:
Our place was no longer ours to use.

OH, OH, OH

She does not ask what she
Might need from my touch.
She turns away from me.
Watch all the resilient weeds:

How they wither will say how sour
The ground has become, walked over
By love and follower. See
The spaces between the trees,

Crossed by flitting things: poorwills,
Sparrows, while I wish for sameness:
Of life and love, and being loved.
I bet in town the people get to dawn

And say to know is thought's arthritis,
Say it is better to walk through leaves,
Better that she turns and I follow
Between the oaks in the old oak grove.

MILL CREEK

He pulled the tractor over, set the brake
And gripped his chest. That old marine
Died hauling two more apple crates
Back to the mill. The way the juice came, clean

As clear honey—my brothers and me
Would get five bucks picking the trees twisted
Into the small orchards that he
Kept along ponds or wedged amid

The broad crops of the bigger farms.
Once, he gave me an extra five
To pull up a drowned goose, in my bare arms—
Its wings extended like it was alive,

In take off. It swayed in the current,
Head drooped at the end of its neck,
The black leather bill bent
Down towards bottom. Other geese, one duck

Stood on rocks all around, each
Face pointed, pointing in a different direction.
When you worked, he would teach
All about the cider. Ultra violet irradiation

Cleaned it as it ran, sweet at the tap.
You'd stand beside the flats, soggy,
Mealy with apple pulp. The paper cup
Seemed filled with froth. He'd say, *See?*

The foam is all apple sugar,
The ex-marine. Stern. Demanding attention.
He'd scoop the bubbles to his mouth on his finger,
Hand you the cup, saying *Taste it again.*

FRAGMENT IX:
THE LOVER'S ASSERTION

Think of the landowner
In the wasteland, her face worn
By the white sun which culls water,

Turns soil sand. That ground
She tucked her child into,
Wrapped in rotted cardboard.

Out there, she wakes and sleeps,
Sleeps, wakes and stares out:
Our luck is a dear thing.

And the religions confuse:
Blood slicks the hardwood
In one house, another house burns.

And what is precious? Not years.
We batter at the portals
Of what is precious.

Sustain our love. Beat at the fastened
Door of the closed vault.
Think what might be locked away in that heart-place.

WINTER CROPLAND

I fled the devil
Where he stood
Among the turning crows
Over the tired field. *Caw*
They call. They call,
I feel an answer in me,
Gathered in my stomach:
I am made
Of a terrible substance,
Old, hotter
Than the dribbling shit
Of fever. Strangling
Deliverer, I am brittle.
Bright-Finger, I am
A grafting, a child.
Cloak me, father.
Mother, love me:
I have done wrong.
Corn stubble stuck
In crusted snow,
Row on row of corn
Through which the crows
Caw and pick, crush
Kernels pinched
In black beaks, flat-
Black, like the cleft
Of a goat's hoof.
My mouth tastes too much of salt.

POTATO GRADER ELEGY

No engine. No belt-drive. Even then
Wayne county people wouldn't spend
Money to burn gas. No: for a few blisters,
With a little muscle ache,
For a few dark mornings in the weeks after the digging,

They could do it themselves: no sense
In being wasteful.

We climbed down the hay-chute
Into the basement of the barn,
Dropped to the floor, straddled the manure gutter
Behind the stanchions, the water dishes
Rusted stuck on their pivots.

We crawled over mounds of clapboard:
Kindling for the winter, nails popping in the fire.
Simple. A hand-crank. The flat planes

Of the roller first kinked, then caught
The chain-link track, the conveyor.
I turned the handle. My little brother rode the belt,
Arms up to keep his fingers clear of the rollers.
Hopped off at the other end.

Baby reds and fingerlings would've fallen through
And gathered underneath.

Grade A's would make it, be collected
In a rough sack, sold for little. The people before us
Knew not to want more than you can have.
He has been ashes for eight years. I never learn.
I like the things that keep me big:

Pizza, white cake, cold bottles of good beer,
Late conversations, little sleep.
He is where he is. I keep what I can.

PIERCE-ARROW LIMOUSINE

The wooden dash powders
As you thumb the dry rot.

The cracking rubber tires harrumph
Against the floor like

The skin around the mouth
Of a Basset hound.

Horsehair molds in steel springs,
Black and viscid inside the rear seat.

One swatch of leather strapping still
Laced through the latch dangles from the fender.

You try now to love those things
That waste can only slowly undo.

TRANSMISSION

Strange, working
With the old man again:

Don't own tools. Don't fix things.

The smell of burnt oil, tires
That need to be patched,

Sawdust slumped in buckets
Waiting for some carelessness
To clean up.

Breaker bar, he says

And twists the bolts that hold
The parts that don't work anymore.

CRUSH HOKUM

I walked in want of comfort for my heart
Whose rude erratic language I heard thunk
And plunge with me towards town in summer's heat.

A storm-felled tree that spanned from bank to bank
Believed me when I laid on it and wailed
Into its bark. A dream where my heart sank

Beneath brown floods came back and sped
Me from the spot into the underbrush.
I crawled until I'd left the cold brook's sound,

And soon enough the day took on the hush
Of really middle places, where deer stands
Dangle from muddled oaks beneath a crush

Of clouds so bright they terrify—the bands
Of glowing blue which showed between in shocks
Of shape consoled me as I wrung my hands

To Rubik's cube my heart back into place.
When the woods gave way to the pruned orchard
I lay down in the pick-up matted grass.

RECUSATIO

Hemlock cleaves to our breath when we ask.

Still, we listen everywhere and say
Tell me the world. We search the books

And say *Tell me the world.*

*

Walk with the one you love
Through the leaves,
Beside the water. Declare:

We will not know the world

As the sentence that is your life
Courses towards its end. It is only one
In a story not ever to be read.

GRATITUDE

My thanks are especially owed to my mother and father, whose conviction that one must lead one's own life has inspired my course. And to Stephanie Wallace, whose constancy has prepared and encouraged me, and uplifts me, always.

I am forever grateful to the teachers who gave poetry to me: Robert Pinsky, Karl Kirchwey, and Maggie Dietz, James Longenbach, MJ Iuppa, and Bill Waddell, and Tony Leuzzi are among them.

I am thankful for the comradeship and deep listening offered to me by Joseph Spece. Finally, I offer thanks to Kiel M. Gregory and CJ Southworth, whose attentiveness and labor have made this book possible.

D. Eric Parkison grew up in western New York State. He received his MA in English from the University of Rochester, and his MFA in Poetry from Boston University. He lives in Lynn, MA.

Made in the USA
Monee, IL
06 December 2020

51415677R00033